Families

Brothers and Sisters

Rebecca Rissman

Heinemann Library
Chicago, Illinois

www.heinemannraintree.com
Visit our website to find out more information about Heinemann-Raintree books.

To order:
☎ Phone 888-454-2279
💻 Visit www.heinemannraintree.com to browse our catalog and order online.

Edited by Rebecca Rissman and Catherine Veitch
Designed by Ryan Frieson
Picture research by Tracy Cummins
Originated by Capstone Global Library Ltd
Printed and bound in China by Leo Paper Products Ltd

14 13 12 11 10
10 9 8 7 6 5 4 3 2 1

Library of Congress Cataloging-in-Publication Data
Rissman, Rebecca.
  Brothers and sisters / Rebecca Rissman.
    p. cm.—(Families)
  Includes bibliographical references and index.
  ISBN 978-1-4329-4655-5 (hc)—ISBN 978-1-4329-4663-0 (pb)
  1. Brothers and sisters—Juvenile literature. 2. Families—Juvenile literature. I. Title.
  HQ759.96.R57 2011
  306.875—dc22   2010016990

Acknowledgments
We would like to thank the following for permission to reproduce photographs: Corbis pp. 5 (©Randy Faris), 10 (©Edith Held), 19 (©Image Source) 23 d (Image Source); Getty Images pp. 4 (arabianEye), 8 (Edgardo Contreras), 9 (Karen Moskowitz), 13 (DK Stock/Guillermo Hung), 15 (Ryuichi Sato), 17 (Yellow Dog Productions); istockphoto pp. 6 (©Shelly Perry), 7 (©Gary Sludden), 14 (©James Blinn), 20 (©John Prescott), 21 (©Kristian Sekulic), 22 (©Diane Labombarbe), 23 a (©John Prescott), 23 b (©Shelly Perry); 23 d (© Image Source) Shutterstock pp. 11 (©Jaren Jai Wicklund), 12 (©tonobalaguerf), 16 (©Yuri Arcurs), 18 (©Christopher Futcher), 23 c (©Jaren Jai Wicklund).

Front cover photograph of a brother and sister holding paper figurines reproduced with permission of Getty Images (American Images Inc). Back cover photograph of a brother and sister reproduced with permission of istockphoto (© James Blinn).

We would like to thank Anne Pezalla and Nancy Harris for their invaluable help in the preparation of this book.

Every effort has been made to contact copyright holders of any material reproduced in this book. Any omissions will be rectified in subsequent printings if notice is given to the publisher.

Contents

What Is a Family?

A family is a group of people who care for each other.

Families are made up of different people.

People in families are called
family members.

All families are different.
All families are special.

What Are Families Like?

Families can be big or small.

Families can be loud or quiet.

Brothers and Sisters

brother

sister

There are brothers and sisters in some families.

Brothers and sisters are called siblings.

Girl siblings are called sisters.

Boy siblings are called brothers.

Some brothers and sisters look alike.

Some brothers and sisters
look different.

Some brothers and sisters live with their parents.

Some brothers and sisters live away
from their parents.

Some brothers and sisters share the same parents.

Some brothers and sisters have different parents. They are stepbrothers or stepsisters.

Some brothers and sisters are adopted. They have joined a

new family.

Do you have brothers or sisters?

Family Tree

Mother — Father

Brother   You   Sister

Picture Glossary

 **adopted** invited into a new family. Many families adopt children.

 **member** person who belongs to a group

 **sibling** brother or sister

 **step-brother** or **step-sister** brother or sister with different parents

Index

Note to Parents and Teachers

Before Reading

Explain to children that all families are different. Tell children that some families have only one child, while others have many children. Ask children to name their family members and list any brothers and sisters they might have.

After Reading

• Explain to children that some families adopt children. This means that they welcome a new child into their family. Ask children if they know a family who has adopted a child.

• After reviewing the family tree on page 22, draw a family tree for one volunteer child on the board. Encourage children to go home and draw their own family trees.